Book 4

Comprehension Lifters

Written by Dr. Sheila Twine

Published by World Teachers Press®

Order Number 2-5126
ISBN 1-58324-050-0

A B C D E F 03 02 01 00

Educational Resources
395 Main Street
Rowley, MA 01969
www.worldteacherspress.com

Foreword

Comprehension Lifters is a set of blackline masters designed to assist students who have experienced difficulties with reading and comprehension. Topics are of high interest to appeal to older students with low literacy skills. Comprehension activities are varied and include superficial and in-depth questions requiring students to interact with text at a range of levels.

The four books of *Comprehension Lifters* can be used on their own or in conjunction with the four books of *Literacy Lifters* by the same author. Thus, students working at a basic level on Book 1 of *Literacy Lifters* would progress to Book 1 of *Comprehension Lifters* before moving on to Book 2 of *Literacy Lifters*.

In both *Literacy Lifters* and *Comprehension Lifters*, the book numbers do not correspond to grade or class levels, but rather to the skill level of students. Thus, Book 1 is aimed at a basic reading level and would be suitable for students who had floundered with their start to literacy. Book 2 would be appropriate for students who require assistance with basic skills. Books 3 and 4 would suit students whose reading and understanding of text is at a low level.

About the Author

Dr. Sheila Twine is an educational consultant who has worked with students with special needs, as well parents and teachers, in England, Scotland and Australia. She is the author of three books containing practical techniques for working with students who experience difficulties with reading and spelling. She holds a Master's Degree and a Doctorate in Education.

Dr. Twine has been president of various associations and foundations involved with underachieving students with a variety of disabilities from mild developmental delay to attention deficit disorder. She was principal of a residential remedial primary school and has been the director of an education consultancy for many years.

Contents

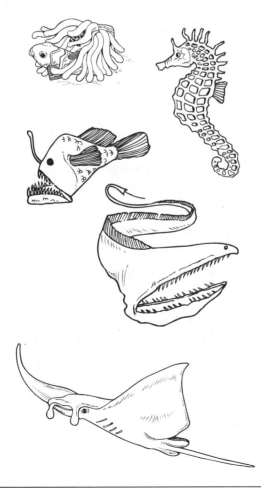

Teachers Notes

GENERAL LAYOUT

Comprehension Lifters has been designed as a teaching tool to assist you in raising the literacy levels of your students who are experiencing difficulties with reading and comprehension.

The page layout is similar throughout the books with text well separated by pictures to make discouraged readers feel more at ease. Each book has forty topic pages dealing with aspects of the same theme which are intended to be of interest to older students with low literacy skills. The font size is appropriate to the students' ages and so is smaller than normal for the easier reading level; therefore, the pages do not look "babyish."

The **Backing Sheet** can be copied on the back of any or all of the topic pages. It is general and designed to complement your teaching. It contains space for activities in word study, integration and writing.

TOPIC PAGES

Each topic page has a number of sections. There is a section for patterned words which are phonically regular (found, sound, round) and for sight words (the, said, enough) for instant recognition. Most pages also have longer words broken into "chunks" to encourage your students to tackle unfamiliar words more easily (nav-i-gate).

There are many comprehension sections. These include:

Main idea – Students need to be able to grasp the main idea of the text. Selecting or creating a title assists with this and is featured on every topic page.

Cloze activity – Each page also features a cloze activity which requires students to think as they read so a sensible word can be inserted into the blank spaces using clues from the text.

Questions – **Literal** questions are included where the answer is clear from the story. There are also **inferential** questions where students are asked to think and provide a logical answer. (He put on his raincoat – What was the weather like?)

Others – Some pages feature **following directions** or **giving opinions**. Some ask students to **make judgements** and some ask for elements to be put in correct **sequence**.

At the bottom of each topic page there is a section that can act as a challenge to the more able students in your group to read to the others. The section either asks a deeper level of comprehension question or gives more information about the topic.

TEACHING TIPS

Two teaching strategies which were used when the layout of the topic pages was being tested were **pre-reading** and **blank-filling**. You may like to try them.

Pre-reading – Students were asked to glance at the pictures on their topic page then turn the page over (so no reading took place). They were then asked to volunteer snippets of information on the topic.

> (It's all about ballooning, My mother went up in a hot-air balloon, They have a fire machine to make the balloon go up, Some balloons go on races, etc.)

This serves to get your students tuned in to the topic. Three things then happen. First, the reading becomes easier (they're expecting the words). Second, their comprehension is better, and third, recall is improved.

Blank-filling – The topic pages are teaching tools for you, so it's a good idea not to let your students fill in the blanks while you are going through the various sections of the page with them. The "pencils down" rule allows them to focus their whole attention on what you're saying. Later comes their turn for practice and activity by filling in the blanks and answering the questions on their own. The **Backing Sheet** can be used while you're teaching. For instance,

> "Let's spell that word together. Now spell it silently, turn over the paper and see if you can write it down."

Teachers Notes

TOPIC PAGES

The **Topic Pages** have been designed for students who are experiencing difficulties with literacy. They aim to create a high level of interest which will appeal to students with low skill levels.

The **Topic Page** layouts have been tested in small remedial groups using an ACTIVE teaching mode which is outlined in the model below. Students were encouraged to fill in "blanks" in the **Topic Pages** only after teaching had taken place. The **Backing Sheet** was used during the teaching for students to write patterned, chunked and sight words from memory. Topics are arranged in themes and each page contains scope for your active teaching as follows:

Pre-reading

• Discovering pre-existing knowledge through discussion, with students volunteering snippets of information after looking at illustrations.

Reading

• Oral, group, silent, paired, or partner reading.

Word Study

• Phonic word patterns of regular words or theme words.

• Chunked words – words broken into chunks to assist blending and spelling rather than conventional syllables.

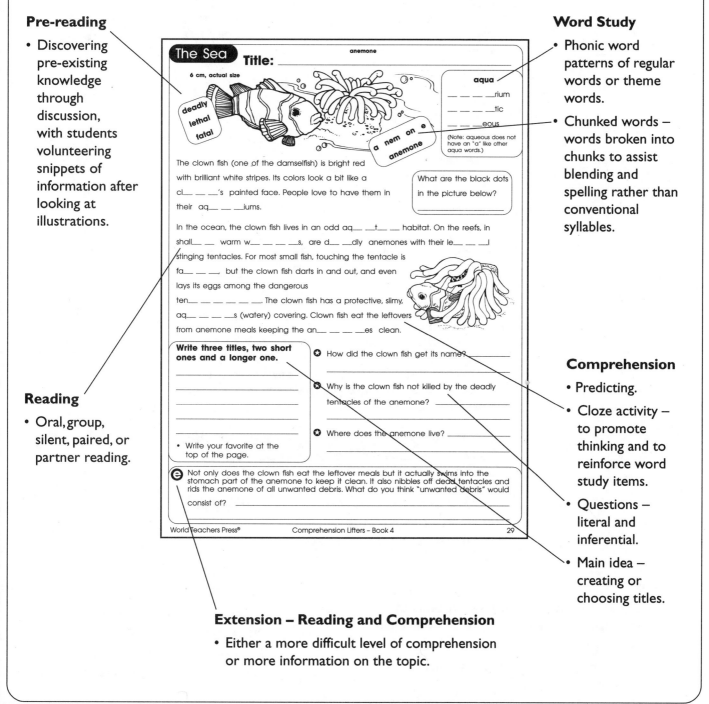

Comprehension

• Predicting.

• Cloze activity – to promote thinking and to reinforce word study items.

• Questions – literal and inferential.

• Main idea – creating or choosing titles.

Extension – Reading and Comprehension

• Either a more difficult level of comprehension or more information on the topic.

Teachers Notes

BACKING SHEET
The **Backing Sheet** is provided for you to copy on the back of any or all of the **Topic Pages**.
You'll notice that it is general and suitable for all **Topic Pages**. It is designed to complement your teaching and you may care to use or adapt the following suggestions as shown on the sample **Backing Sheet**.

Patterned Words
• Can be used while you're teaching or for practice afterwards.

Topic Words
• Practice in reading, oral spelling and writing new topic words.

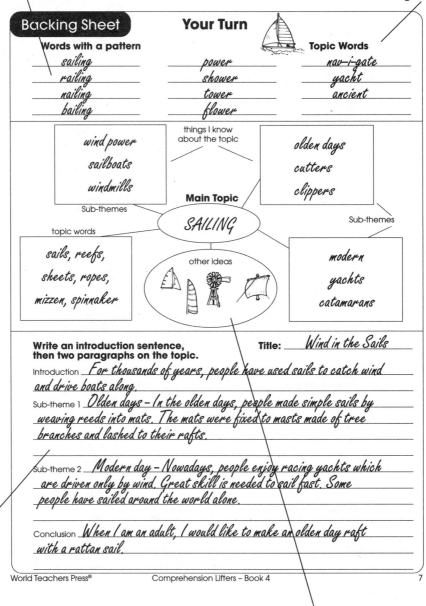

Backing Sheet

Your Turn

Words with a pattern
sailing
railing
nailing
bailing

power
shower
tower
flower

Topic Words
nav-i-gate
yacht
ancient

things I know about the topic

wind power
sailboats
windmills

Sub-themes

olden days
cutters
clippers

Sub-themes

topic words

Main Topic

SAILING

sails, reefs,
sheets, ropes,
mizzen, spinnaker

other ideas

modern
yachts
catamarans

Write an introduction sentence, then two paragraphs on the topic.

Title: _Wind in the Sails_

Introduction _For thousands of years, people have used sails to catch wind and drive boats along._

Sub-theme 1 _Olden days – In the olden days, people made simple sails by weaving reeds into mats. The mats were fixed to masts made of tree branches and lashed to their rafts._

Sub-theme 2 _Modern day – Nowadays, people enjoy racing yachts which are driven only by wind. Great skill is needed to sail fast. Some people have sailed around the world alone._

Conclusion _When I am an adult, I would like to make an olden day raft with a rattan sail._

World Teachers Press®   Comprehension Lifters – Book 4   7

Writing
• Written (factual material) can assist students to write in a logical, thematic structure by giving them a standard format to formulate good habits.

• Later, format can be extended as basic skill improves and is wellfounded.

Integration
• Combining elements from text with pre-existing knowledge.

• Practice in sorting out random thoughts into sub-themes, lists, or categories.

Backing Sheet

Your Turn

Words with a pattern

_____

_____

_____

_____

_____

_____

_____

_____

Topic Words

_____

_____

_____

_____

things I know about the topic

Sub-themes

Main Topic

topic words

other ideas

Sub-themes

Write an introduction sentence, then two paragraphs on the topic.

Title: _____

Introduction _____

_____

Sub-theme 1 _____

_____

_____

_____

Sub-theme 2 _____

_____

_____

Conclusion _____

_____

Program Overview

Page	Subject	Word Study	Feature	Word Count
9	Pinnipeds	bi, tri, quad	main idea	81
10	Sea Horse	synonyms	listing	78
11	Crabs	cea, cient, cial	deca, octo	83
12	Hydrofoil	ce	experiment	71
13	Polar Bears	ce, ci, cy	clues	89
14	Pacific Ocean	ge, ce, ci	words in quotes	88
15	Ocean Trenches	theme words	main idea	87
16	Dolphins	ph, ci	words in quotes	96
17	Blue Whale	ge, gi	true/false/doesn't say	101
18	Letter	–	clues	100
19	Submarine	sion, sure	inference	100
20	Making a Submarine	–	following directions	101
21	Hovercraft	sign	inference	100
22	Catamaran	cious	inference	107
23	Shore Fishing	synonyms	inference	96
24	Big Game Fishing	ex	inference	97
25	Ichthyosaur	suffixes	make a poster	66
26	Pleurosaurus	theme words	comparisons	101
27	Jellyfish	synonyms	odd title	90
28	Prize Letter	synonyms	clues	97
29	Clown Fish	aqua	short/long titles	106
30	Ancient Egyptian Craft	cient, cious, cial	inference	98
31	Endeavour	tion	pace out dimensions	101
32	Victory	ory, ary, ery	title/subtitle	98
33	Pollution	tion	make a poster	99
34	Exxon Valdez	or, zeroes	listing	104
35	Oil	suffixes	make a poster	108
36	Oil Rigs	word building	listing	103
37	Sharks	ci, ce	frightening title	106
38	Red and White Muscles	ue, synonyms	word in quotes	103
39	Fish Movement	wr	inference	109
40	Turtles	theme words	true/false/doesn't say	106
41	Navigation	tele, tion	inference	92
42	Making a Compass	silent "w"	sequence	106
43	Weapons	ea	headline	103
44	Punishment at Sea	dis, ful	inference	104
45	Marie Celeste	theme words	mysterious titles	105
46	Pirates	synonyms, cious	interesting titles	106
47	Pirate's Map	ough, ight	draw from directions	124
48	Bird Migration	word building	opinion	116

Title: _____

sep ar ate
separate

ped

bi__ __ __

quadru__ __ __

pinni__ __ __

tripod

krill
1 – 3 cm long

People are bip__ __s, which means they have two f__ __t. Most animals are

qu__ __ __ __ __ __ __s, which means they ha__ __ __ __ __ __ __ f__ __t. Seals and

walruses don't have separ__ __ __d feet with legs like we have. They are called

p__ __ __ __ __ __ __s. Their feet are pinned together. Pi__ __ __ __ __d actually

means "fin foot." Sea lions are also p__ __ __ __ __ __ __s. All pin__ __ __ __ __s are

mammals so they need to __ __ea__ __e air, and they suckle their young on rich milk.

They eat small fish or krill and live mostly in the colder oceans.

Think of two titles that give the main idea of the article.

_____

_____

_____

_____

• Write the best at the top of the page.

✪ Krill are like small shrimp. | True | False |

✪ Write three types of pinniped.

_____ , _____

and _____

✪ What does pinniped mean? _____

✪ How can you remember the word? _____

_____

e Krill are eaten by many whales, sea birds, penguins and pinnipeds. Krill numbers are becoming less year by year. Scientists think global warming may be the reason. What do you think will happen if too many krill disappear?_____

_____

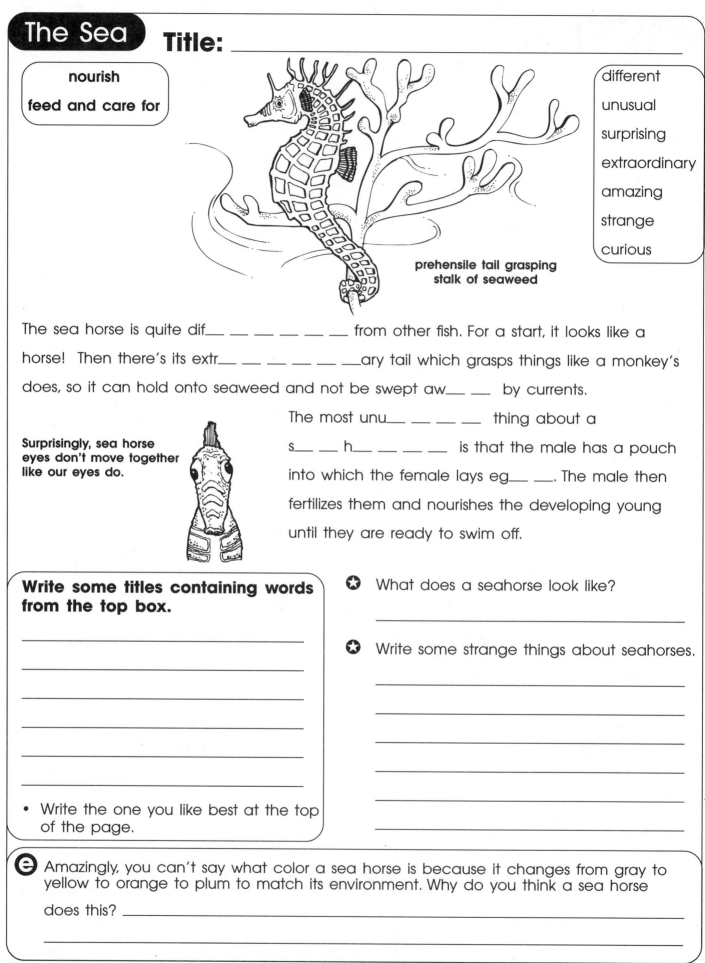

The Sea

Title: _____

nourish

feed and care for

different
unusual
surprising
extraordinary
amazing
strange
curious

prehensile tail grasping
stalk of seaweed

The sea horse is quite dif__ __ __ __ __ __ from other fish. For a start, it looks like a

horse! Then there's its extr__ __ __ __ __ __ary tail which grasps things like a monkey's

does, so it can hold onto seaweed and not be swept aw__ __ by currents.

Surprisingly, sea horse eyes don't move together like our eyes do.

The most unu__ __ __ __ thing about a

s__ __ h__ __ __ __ is that the male has a pouch

into which the female lays eg__ __. The male then

fertilizes them and nourishes the developing young

until they are ready to swim off.

Write some titles containing words from the top box.

_____

_____

_____

_____

_____

_____

• Write the one you like best at the top of the page.

✪ What does a seahorse look like?

_____

✪ Write some strange things about seahorses.

_____

_____

_____

_____

_____

_____

e Amazingly, you can't say what color a sea horse is because it changes from gray to yellow to orange to plum to match its environment. Why do you think a sea horse

does this? _____

_____

Title: _____

legs/pod

feet/ped

deca = ten

decapod = ten legs

tripod = ____ legs

octopod = _____

quadruped = _____

biped = _____

sounds like sh

cea

o__ __ __n

crusta__ __ __n

cial

spe__ __ __ __

so__ __ __ __

sounds like ch

cient

an__ __ __ __ __

effi__ __ __ __

Crabs belong to the class called "crus__ __ __ __ __ __." They live on the tidal flats of our seas and o__ __ __ __s. They are called deca__ __ __s because they have __ __ __ __ __ __s. Their front legs are clawed and they use the cl__ __ __ for feeding and fighting. Some spec__ __ __ crabs are called "fiddler crabs." In the male crab, the front claw is waved about to attract females or to menace and fight other males. The huge claw looks like a fiddle and the small one is like a bow.

Four words are often sufficient for a title.

☐ Crab Legs and Claws

☐ Crabs have Ten Legs and are called Decapods

☐ Fiddler Crabs have a Huge Claw to Wave

☐ Attracting Females

• Pick the best title and write it at the top of the page.

★ Which class do crabs belong to?

_____

★ How did the fiddler crab get its name?

_____

_____

★ What does the fiddler crab use its huge claw for?

_____

_____

e Crabs are a truly ancient class of animals. Crab-like creatures have lived on Earth for about 650,000,000 (650 million) years. The world's largest crab is the giant spider crab off the coast of Japan. Its shell is 30 cm across and its legs can stretch over 2 meters!

What do you think "truly" means in this paragraph? _____

_____

Title: _____

in ven tion
invention

ce

__ __rtain
pri__ __
ra__ __s
__ __nter
pie__ __s
pier__ __
for__ __

Hydrofoil type of boat

Ships have to for__ __ their way through water. This slows them down and raises the pri__ __ of travel. A clever invention was the hy__ __ __fo__ __. This kind of boat has "wings" under the water. When the boat reaches a __ __rtain speed, the hy__ __ __foils provide lift.

Up comes the hull and the boat ra__ __s above the water. Now there is much less drag. An aircraft gets lift in the same way. The shape of its wings provides lift as air rac__ __ over them.

Circle the best title.

Wings Under Water   On Top of the Waves

Speeding Along

⭐ Hydrofoils travel above the water. | True | False |

⭐ Why are hydrofoils able to travel faster than most normal boats?

_____

_____

⭐ How is a hydrofoil boat like an aircraft?

_____

_____

ℯ You can make a "wing" with a piece of paper, a drinking straw and some string. Fold the paper in half and push the top half until it bulges, then glue or tape it down. Pierce a hole through both layers for the straw and string. A friend now blows on the curved edge. What happens?

_____

Title: _____

ce
distan__ __
poun__ __
crevi__ __
enfor__ __d
__ __ntury
sin__ __

ci	cy
mer__ __	
__ __rcumpolar	
i__ __	

The polar bear is the largest carnivore on land and can weigh up to 600 kg. It lives only in the i__y Arctic areas around the North Pole

circumpolar

(__ __rcumpol__ __). It is not found at the South P__ __ __. Polar b__ __ __ __ are strong swim__ers and can run as fast as 40 km/h, but only for short dist__ __ __ __s. Their diet consists mainly of fish and seals. The seals are pounced on when they come up through holes in the i__ __ to brea__ __e. They will also eat vegetation during the short Arctic summ__ __.

Range of polar bear

Circle the two best titles.
Write one at the top of the page.

- Seals for Lunch
- Circumpolar Carnivore
- Arctic Summer
- Polar Bears
- A Crevice in the Ice

✪ How heavy is a large polar bear? _____

✪ Can polar bears run a long way? _____

What was your clue? _____

_____

✪ How do they catch their meals? _____

_____

---

e During this century, polar bear numbers dropped to around 5,000, but since new hunting regulations have been enforced, the numbers have now risen to around 40,000. However, the effects of pollution may now...

_____

_____.

Title: _____

The Pa__ __fic Ocean is the lar__ __st ocean on Ear__ __. It covers one third of our planet's surf__ __ __ and is bigger than all the other oceans put together. The Pa__ __ __ __c is also the ocean with the greatest aver__ __ __ depth. Ocean trenches plun__ __ to eleven kilometers below the surf__ __ __ of the water.

Pacific Ocean

Equator

Australia

hard "ge"

ra__ __

avera__ __

lar__ __st

plun__ __

submer__ __d

dama__ __

soft "ce" or "ci"

for__ __

fier__ __ly

surfa__ __

pea__ __ful

Pa__ __fic

en__ __rcling

It has many submer__ __ __ volcanoes and many that have "built" islands which now have coral r__ __fs enc__ __ __ling them.

Though Pac__ __ __ __ means "peaceful," occasionally fier__ __ storms of great for__ __ can ra__ __ over the ocean, and dama__ __ ships and shores.

✪ How much of the Earth's surface does the Pacific Ocean cover? _____

✪ The Pacific is not always peaceful. What sometimes happens?

_____

_____

✪ Why is the word "built" in quotation marks? _____

_____

Choose two titles which give the main idea.

☐ Submerged Volcanoes

☐ Earth's Largest Ocean

☐ Fierce Storms

☐ Ocean Trenches

☐ Ring of Fire

☐ Pacific Ocean

• Write one at the top of the page.

e The Pacific rim is called "The Ring of Fire" because of its many volcanoes and earthquakes. Cracks in the Earth's crust around the edge of the Pacific plate allow molten rock and hot gases to escape.

Do you think "Ring of Fire" is a good name? _____ Why? _____

_____

The Sea

Title: _____

deep ocean

tr__ __ __ __

submerged

v__ __ __ __ __ __ __

trenches
sulphur
gases
pressure
descended
variety

In some parts of our oceans there are deep valleys or cracks called "trenches." In the deepest tre__ __ __ __s, where the Earth's crust is weak or cracked, hot sulphurous gas__ __ escape into the water. Sometimes the water actually boils. It's pitch black, and water pressu__ __ at these depths is crushing. Surely no life could exist.

However, in 1977, scientists desc__ __ __ed two and a half kilometers and discovered a var__ __ __ __ of life. There were giant tube worms, blind crabs, sea anemones, fish and eels which glowed in the darkness.

✪ What are ocean trenches? _____
_____

✪ Is there any light in the deepest parts of the ocean?

| Yes | No |

If no, why not? _____
_____

If you said yes, where does the light come from?

_____

✪ What does the word descend mean? _____

_____

Write a variety of titles giving the main idea.

_____
_____
_____
_____
_____

e Way back in 1960, the "Trieste" was the first submersible with people aboard to descend 11 km to the deepest trench on Earth. The crew saw living creatures even there. These ate tiny creatures who lived on the gases and bacteria coming from the interior of the Earth. Try to describe conditions way down there.

Title: _____

ci

spe__ __al

so__ __able

spe__ __es

whistles

school

echoes

ph

dol__ __ins

__ __otogra__ __

__ __ysical

geogra__ __y

telegra__ __

tele__ __one

Dol__ __ins belong to the same order of animals as whales. The order is called

"cetacea" (set ay sea ah). There are a few spe__ __es of dol__ __ __ __s. The

bottle-nosed dolphin seems happy to swim around people and close to sho__ __. It's a

playful, __ __ysical animal, often leaping and rolling. Dolphins are soc__ __ __

animals and live in small sch__ __ __s, called pods.

People love to snap __ __otogr__ __ __s of these intelligent, friendly creatures.

Dol__ __ __ __ __ telegr__ __ __ messages to each other in a series of clicks and

whistles. E__ __oes from whis__ __ __s bouncing back

from solid objects help d__ __ __ __ __ __s find fish and

squid to e__ __.

dolphin "aunts" help
at the birth of a calf

Which is the best phrase for a title?

☐ Dolphins and Whales

☐ A Dolphin's Life

☐ Fish and Squid

☐ Physical and Social

☐ Clicks and Whistles

✪ What is the order that whales and dolphins belong to?

_____

✪ What do you think a dolphin "aunt" is, and how do they help?

_____

_____

✪ How do dolphins "talk" to each other? _____

_____

ⓔ The geographical range of dolphins is the warmer waters of the world. The chief threat to dolphins is the driftnet from fishing boats. Entanglement in these nets means that dolphins can't surface and so they drown. Sharks and killer whales also prey on dolphins.

On the back of the sheet, write your solution to the driftnet fishing danger.

Title: _____

person
1.8 m

blue whale
25 m

The blue whale is the largest animal on land or sea. It makes an elephant look small. It is bigger than the lar__ __st dinosaur we have yet found. A hu__ __ adult can weigh 120,000 kg but are __ __nerally between 80,000 kg and 110,000 kg. What do you weigh? _____

The ran__ __ of the blue whale is around the North and South Poles (though it swims to warmer waters for the birth of a calf).

For such a __ __gant__ __ animal, it eats tiny marine creatures, which it "sieves" through the bristles of its "baleen," after taking in a mouthful of krill-laden water.

ge
__ __ntle
ran__ __
endan__ __red
__ __nerally
hu__ __
lar__ __st

gi
tra__ __c
__ __ant
__ __gantic

baleen instead of teeth

Write some titles using the words in the top box.

_____

_____

_____

_____

_____

_____

• Write your favorite at the top of the page.

✪ The blue whale is the largest creature on Earth.

| True | False | Doesn't say |

✪ What is a baby whale called? _____

✪ What do you think krill is? _____
_____

✪ How does this whale eat? _____
_____

e So many blue whales were killed that numbers dropped to a tragic 1,000 animals which made it one of the most endangered species. They have been given international protection since 1966. Apart from hunting, what could pose a danger to whale numbers? _____

_____

_____

Title: _____

From this short letter we can find lots of clues to guide our thinking.

> Craggy Point
> Coast Shore, CA
> May 16, 1998
>
> Dear Jim,
>
> Just a note to say that I'll meet you at the 4:30 train Friday evening at Rockhampton Junction around 6 p.m.
>
> Bring your swim suit and climbing boots. I still have your fishing rod and that old guitar for you to strum. The baby eagles have flown and our friendly pod of dolphins is still in the bay so bring your snorkel.
>
> You'll be pleased to know that I've found where the hens are laying!
>
> Jo Jo sends a hug and is looking forward to seeing you again.
>
> Love,
> Uncle Andrew

✪ What sort of area does Uncle Andrew live in?

_____

Clue: _____

✪ What season of the year is it? _____

Clue: _____

✪ How old do you think Jim is? (3 – 5 years, 6 – 9 years, 10 – 12 years, 13 – 15 years) _____

Clue: _____

✪ How is Jim traveling? _____ Clue: _____

_____

✪ How long do you think he is staying? _____

✪ Has he visited before? _____ Clue: _____

_____

✪ Who is Jo Jo? _____ Clue: _____

✪ Does Uncle Andrew live alone? (apart from Jo Jo and the hens) _____

Clue: _____

✪ What will be on the menu? _____ Clue: _____

✪ What will Jim and Uncle Andrew do during the day? _____

_____

✪ During the evening? _____

Title: _____

sion

deci__ __ __ __

suspen__ __ __ __

explo__ __ __ __s

sure

pres__ __ __ __

__ __ __ __ly

long

elongated

torpedo

Subm__ __ __ __ __s were developed as machines of war. They destroyed many ships in

both World Wars (1914–18 and 1939–45). Elong__ __ __ __ bombs called

tor__ __ __ __es were fired, causing expl__ __ __ __ __s in the ships they hit.

up periscope

Subm__ __ __ __ __ __ have strong hulls to withstand

the great water pres__ __ __ __ in deep dives. When

a deci__ __ __ __ is made to dive, sea water is

allowed to fill ballast tanks making the sub heavier.

When the deci__ __ __ __ is made to surface, air is

forced under pres__ __ __ __ into the t__ __ks,

making the s__ __ __ __rine light__ __. So, a sub stays

in suspen__ __ __ __ at a chosen depth because of

the balance between ballast and air.

Make a decision and write the best title at the top of the page.

☐ Deep Dives

☐ Both World Wars

☐ Water Pressure

☐ Submarines

☐ Ballast Tanks

✪ Why were submarines developed? _____

_____

✪ What do you think "periscope depth" means? _____

_____

_____

✪ How is a submarine prepared for diving? _____

_____

_____

ⓔ Submersibles are tiny submarines which can take two or three people to ocean depths with cameras, viewing windows and claws to pick up objects from the ocean floor. On the back of the sheet, describe what you might see from a submersible.

The Sea

Title: _____

your submarine

bottle top

straw with a bend

plastic tube

You'll need:
- plastic soft drink bottle with lid
- small stones or marbles
- a length of plastic tubing or a straw with a bend
- scissors

Let's see how air pressure and ballast can raise or lower a submarine.

Cut two sections from the sides of the bottle near the base. Fill the base with stones or marbles.

Put the bottle upright into a bucket of water. Then screw the lid on tight.

Now feed the tubing or straw into one of the holes you cut and blow air into the bottle. The air will replace some of the water and make your "submarine" lighter so it will rise. To make your sub__ __ __ __ __ __ sink again, simply unscrew the bottle t__ __ and let some of the air esc__ __ __.

✪ What are you using as ballast? _____

_____

✪ What makes your "submarine" lighter? _____

_____

_____

✪ How do you make it sink again? _____

_____

_____

ⓔ Cartesian Diver – Draw some water into a medicine dropper until it floats in a glass of water. Now fill a soft drink bottle, put in your "diver" and screw the lid on tightly.

Squeeze the bottle. What happens? _____

_____

Let it go. What happens? _____

Why? _____

_____

Title: _____

propeller

knots

rudder

sign

de__ __ __ __

de__ __ __ __ing

rede__ __ __ __ed

re__ __ __ __

re__ __g__ation

hovercraft floating at rest

rubber skirt

move
movement
motion

Do hoverc__ __ __ __ float or fly? Planes fly and

boats fl__ __ __. A h__ __ __ __craft is a boat so it

must float. Or does it?

When hovercraft are not moving or only moving slowly,

they certainly do fl__ __ __. However, when they are in

mot__ __ __ they fly!

flying forward ⟶

How does this happen?

Hovercraft are de__ __g__ed with a rubber skirt. Powerful engines push air downwards.

cushion of air

The skirt traps most of the air and lifts the craft up to three meters above the

w__t__ __.

Propellers on deck are des__ __ __ __d to provide forw__ __ __ thrust.

The hov__ __cr__ __ __ is now "flying" over the w__v__s at speeds up to seventy knots.

Decide on the best title.

☐ Rubber Skirts

☐ Float or Fly

☐ Hovercraft

☐ Propellers

☐ Forward Thrust

✪ Why is this craft called a hovercraft?_____

_____

✪ What is the rubber skirt for? _____

_____

✪ When does the hovercraft float and when does it fly?

_____

_____

_____

✪ What does "in motion" mean? _____

---

e The hull of a boat causes a lot of drag as it forces its way through the water. This slows the craft and uses a great deal of power. Inventors have tried many ways of raising hulls of boats out of the water.

Hydrofoils, hovercrafts and catamarans are the results.

What do you think are the benefits? _____

_____

Title: _____

passenger area

cargo level

long, narrow hull of catamaran

cious
pre__ __ __ __ __
spa__ __ __ __ __
atro__ __ __ __ __
deli__ __ __ __ __
suspi__ __ __ __ __

Cata__ __ __ __ __s have two narrow hulls at each side of a spa__ __ __ __ __ boat deck. Some cat__ __ __ __ __ __s are the size of a soccer field and so can carry quantities of pre__ __ __us, weighty cargo such as trucks and machinery. Passengers have plenty of space to stroll about and can eat deli__ __ __ __s meals in spac__ __ __ __ comfort.

Even with high waves and atro__ __ __ __ __ weather, catamarans are quite stable because of their narrow hulls spaced wide apart. Seasickness is rare on cats. The narrow hu__ __s do not have to use as much force to push through the water as normal wide hulls do, so cats can travel fa__ __er and use less engine power.

front view

✪ What is the name of the type of boat with two narrow hulls? _____

✪ Why is seasickness rare on cats? _____ _____

✪ Why can cats travel faster than most boats of the same size? _____ _____

Write a couple of titles.

_____

_____

_____

_____

ⓔ In 1990, the British catamaran Hoverspeed won a speed competition by crossing the Atlantic Ocean in under three and a half days. She traveled at an average speed of thirty-six knots with a top speed of over forty-two knots. Trimarans have three narrow hulls. What are the benefits of multi-hulled ships? Find out and write them on the back of this sheet.

Title: _____

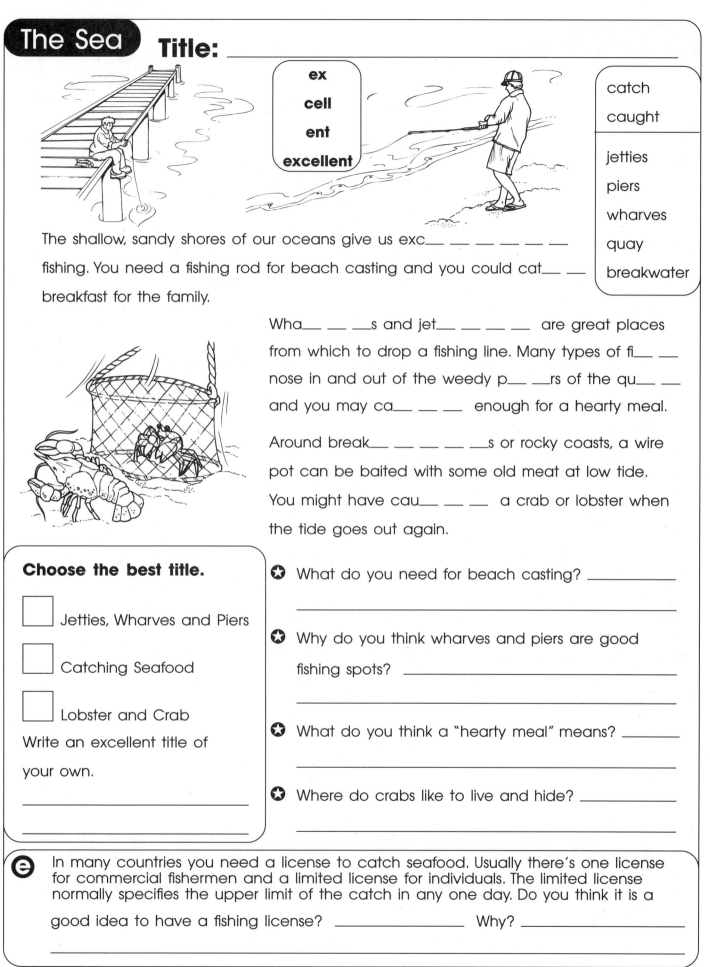

ex

cell

ent

excellent

catch

caught

jetties

piers

wharves

quay

breakwater

The shallow, sandy shores of our oceans give us exc__ __ __ __ __ __ fishing. You need a fishing rod for beach casting and you could cat__ __ breakfast for the family.

Wha__ __ __s and jet__ __ __ __ are great places from which to drop a fishing line. Many types of fi__ __ nose in and out of the weedy p__ __rs of the qu__ __ and you may ca__ __ __ enough for a hearty meal.

Around break__ __ __ __ __s or rocky coasts, a wire pot can be baited with some old meat at low tide. You might have cau__ __ __ a crab or lobster when the tide goes out again.

Choose the best title.

☐ Jetties, Wharves and Piers

☐ Catching Seafood

☐ Lobster and Crab

Write an excellent title of your own.

_____

✪ What do you need for beach casting? _____

_____

✪ Why do you think wharves and piers are good fishing spots? _____

_____

✪ What do you think a "hearty meal" means? _____

_____

✪ Where do crabs like to live and hide? _____

_____

e In many countries you need a license to catch seafood. Usually there's one license for commercial fishermen and a limited license for individuals. The limited license normally specifies the upper limit of the catch in any one day. Do you think it is a good idea to have a fishing license? _____ Why? _____

_____

Title: _____

equip

__ __ __ __ __ment

photo

__ __ __ __ __graphed

The person fishing is strapped in a harness at the stern.

ex

__ __citement

__ __cess

__ __cellent

__ __ercise

__ __tremely

__ __pensive

__ __aggerate

Around the world, people enjoy the excit__ __ __ __ __ of big game

fishing. This is an exp__ __ __ive hobby as it needs a boat with both

comfort and modern equi__ __ __ __ __.

Game fishing is hard work and the person fishing is strapped into a harness so that he or

she is not pulled ov__ __bo__ __ __. Winches are used to land large, heavy fish. An

excel__ __ __ __ crew is needed to manage the boat and help with the fish__ __ __

tackle.

Tuna and shark fishing produces extre__ __ __ __ large fish and

people like to be photo__ __ __ __ __ed with their catch to

prove they did not exa__ __ __ __ __ __ __ its size!

✪ What equipment is needed for game fishing?

_____

_____

Write two titles. Choose the best for the top of the page.

_____

_____

_____

_____

✪ Why do you think it is called "big game fishing"?

_____

_____

✪ Why do people have their photos taken with their

catch? _____

_____

e People can enter "tag and release" competitions for prizes for the weight of fish caught. They simply land their catch and weigh and measure it. They then put a numbered tag on the fish before returning it to the water. These competitions help researchers find out how far fish swim and how long they live. Each time a tagged fish is recaught it adds to our knowledge.

What else can we learn from the tag? _____

_____

Title: _____

showing skeleton of ichthyosaur — dorsal fin like shark

act u al
act u al ly

bony sockets for large eyes

arms and fingers modified into a flipper

history

— — — — — — ~~✗~~ ic

pre— — — — — — _ic

extinct

— — — — — — _ion

fossil

— — — — — — _ized

Ichthyosaur (ik thee a sore) means "fish lizard" from Greek.

This pre__ __ __ __ __ __ __ __ fish-like creature lived in the

sea but it was act__ __ __ __y an air-breathing reptile. Its

diet consisted of fish and squid-like creat__ __ __s which it crunched then swallowed in

big chunks without chewing, much like a modern dolphin does.

We know a great deal about ich__ __ __ __ __ __ __ __ because many almost

complete foss__ __ __ __ed skeletons have been found in England and Germany.

We know:

- It grew up to 2.5 m in length.
- It was ext__ __ __ __ before the dinos__ __ __ __ were.
- It swam like a fish, waving its tail from side to side.

We think:

- It weighed up to 150 kg.
- It didn't hear very well.
- It had live young.

lived 200 million years ago

✪ What did ichthyosaur eat? _____

and _____

✪ How did it eat? _____

_____

Make a poster about the ichthysaur. Give it a heading. Write three headings here then choose the best one.

_____

_____

_____

_____

✪ Did it lay eggs? | Yes | No | Not sure |

What was your clue? _____

✪ Why do we know a lot about ichthyosaur?

_____

_____

🄴 The first fossils of ichthyosaur were found in the late 1800s and it was first thought to be an extinct fish.

As more perfect specimens were located, it was realized that it was actually an air-breathing reptile whose ancestors were land-based animals. Why was it thought to be a fish?

_____

Title: _____

hatchlings

survival

adulthood

scurry

extinction

crocodile

swimmer

130 million years ago

Pleurosaurus (Ploo roh) means "water lizard" and it lived in shallow inland seas. It measured about 1.5 m and was an excellent s__ __ __mer. It looked like a small cr__ __odile but with smoother skin. Its teeth sloped backward, like a shark's, for catching and eating fish.

We know it laid about forty eggs on land and then left its eggs to hatch on their own, like a modern turtle.

The ha__ __ __lings would have to scu__ __y down to the water before being eaten. Once in the water they had to hide in the weeds to avoid being eaten, so only a few sur__ __ __ed into a__ __ __thood.

Write three titles each containing the main idea of the article.

_____

_____

_____

_____

_____

_____

- Write the best title at the top of the page.

✪ How was the pl__ __ __ __saurus like...

a shark? _____

_____

a turtle? _____

_____

a crocodile? _____

_____

✪ Circle 130 million years ago.

130,000   130,000,000   1,300,000   13,000,000

ⓔ Currently skeletons of pleurosaurus have been found only in Europe. The best preserved have come from France. We think it lived at the end of the Jurassic period and into the Cretaceous.

Why do you think it became extinct? _____

_____

Title: _____

venomous
poisonous

float blown up

curious
queer
odd
funny
puzzling
peculiar
strange

stinging tentacles

in hab it ants
inhabitants

Curi__ __ __ inhab__ __ __ ts of the ocean are a group of jellyfish named

"Portuguese man-of-war." One type is called "bluebottle" because of its blue color

and its od__ habit of filling with air to float on top of the waves looking

like bo__ __les.

Another pecu__ __ __ __ thing is the jackfish that

swims among the pois__ __ous tenta__ __ __ __ and

seems to be immune to the venom. When other small

fish see the jackfish amo__ __ the waving tentacles they

think it's safe. Then the small fish are stung and eaten and the

jackfish gets the leftovers.

✪ One sort of Portuguese man-of-war is called

_____

Write an odd title.

_____

_____

Write a straightforward one.

_____

_____

• Write the one you like best at the top of the page.

✪ Write a couple of strange things about this creature.

1. _____

_____

2. _____

_____

✪ What reward does the jackfish receive?

_____

e The Portuguese man-of-war live in large groups in the warm waters round the equator and the tropics.
They drift along being directed by wind and currents like ocean wanderers.

Do you think "ocean wanderer" is a good name? _____ Why? _____

Title: _____

I. A. Thomas
Peak Road
Mt. Sandy, ME

Chicken Roost
PO Box 571
Castine, ME

voyage

cruise

journey

tour

trip

entitles

brochure

luxury

June 25, 1998

Dear Mr. Thomas:

I am writing to confirm your 1st prize win in our Chicken Roost meals drawing.
Congratulations!

The prize ent___ __ __ __s you and a partner to a ten-day voy___ __ __
aboard the lux___ __ __ cruiser "Islander." Your cru___ __ __ starts in Fiji
and tours several islands. The enclosed br___ __ __ure gives details.

Mr. Max Greenwood will contact you to arrange dates and flights to Fiji
where you will spend three nights in a five-star hotel overlooking the bay.
Your spending money of $2,000 will be sent to you three weeks before you
leave.

Yours Sincerely,

J C Smith

J.C. Smith
Promotions Manager

✪ Who won the prize? ☐ Mr. Greenwood   ☐ Mr. Thomas   ☐ Mr. Smith

✪ The prize winner lives in Castine.   ☐ True   ☐ False

✪ What is the word in the letter, meaning "ship"? _____

✪ Why do you think the ship is called "Islander"? _____

_____

✪ What do you think the "details" in the brochure would be? _____

_____

✪ The prize consisted of lots of parts. Write them down.

   e.g., ten-day cruise with partner.   1. _____

   2. _____   3. _____

e There were two conditions regarding the prize. The first was that at least one of the
travelers must be 21 years of age or older. The second was that the trip must be taken
before September 1999.

Do you think these are sensible? _____

Why? _____

The Sea

Title: _____

6 cm, actual size

anemone

deadly
lethal
fatal

a nem on e
anemone

aqua

__ __ __ __rium

__ __ __ __tic

__ __ __eous

(Note: aqueous does not have an "a" like other aqua words.)

The clown fish (one of the damselfish) is bright red with brilliant white stripes. Its colors look a bit like a cl__ __ __'s painted face. People love to have them in their aq__ __ __iums.

What are the black dots in the picture below?

_____

In the ocean, the clown fish lives in an odd aq__ __t__ __ habitat. On the reefs, in shall__ __ warm w__ __ __ __s, are d__ __dly anemones with le__ __ __l stinging tentacles. For most small fish, touching a tentacle is fa__ __ __, but the clown fish darts in and out, and even lays its eggs among the dangerous ten__ __ __ __ __ __. The clown fish has a protective, slimy, aq__ __ __ __s (watery) covering. Clown fish eat the leftovers from anemone meals keeping the an__ __ __ __es clean.

Write three titles, two short ones and a longer one.

_____
_____
_____
_____
_____

• Write your favorite at the top of the page.

✪ How did the clown fish get its name? _____
_____

✪ Why is the clown fish not killed by the deadly tentacles of the anemone? _____
_____

✪ Where does the anemone live? _____
_____

e Not only does the clown fish eat the leftover meals but it actually swims into the stomach part of the anemone to keep it clean. It also nibbles off dead tentacles and rids the anemone of all unwanted debris. What do you think "unwanted debris" would consist of? _____
_____

The Sea

Title: _____

Mediterranean Sea

Egypt

Nile River

ancient

effi__ __ __ __ __ly

suffi__ __ __ __ __

sh sounds with c
precious

deli__ __ __ __ __

spa__ __ __ __ __

social

spe__ __ __ __

offi__ __ __ __ly

Nearly five thousand years ago in An__ __ __ __ __ Egypt, ships were built to carry prec__ __ __ __ cargo across the Medi__ __ __ __ __nean Sea. The spa__ __ __ __ __ craft were made of wooden blocks (like bricks) which were pinned together. Cross benches for oarsmen to sit on held the vessel together. We think only men sailed in those days.

Notice the spe__ __ __ __ "bipod" mast which could be lowered when the ves__ __ __ was under oars. Also note the six oars at the stern which sailors used for effi__ __ __ __ __ steering. There would have been at least twelve oars on each side with an o__ __sman at each oar.

⭐ How old is the boat in the picture? _____

⭐ No one knows how many crew was sufficient to sail the vessel efficiently. What do you think?

oars	_____	sail	_____
steering	_____	officers	_____
extras	_____	Total	_____

(cook, repairs, cargo, extra oarsmen)

⭐ What do you think "bipod" means? _____
_____

Write two special titles describing the main idea.

_____

_____

_____

_____

• Write the one you like best at the top of the page.

e A stone model of an earlier sailing craft was unearthed in Egypt. It is thought to be 11,000 years old and depicts a vessel made of reeds bound together, with a square sail of papyrus (early paper made of reeds). Do you think this craft was for the Nile River or for the sea? _____

Why? _____

The Sea

Title: _____

voyage

journey

expedition

officer's cabins

Cook's "great" cabin

ENDEAVOUR

crew mess room

"sh" sounds

sec**tion**

expedi__ __ __ __

condi__ __ __ __s

mo__ __ __ __

ac__ __ __ __s

spe**cial**

spe**cies**

vi**cious**

atro**cious**

The first exped__ __ __ __ __ of Captain James Cook in the Endeavour lasted three years, from 1768 to 1771. The ship, with ninety-four sailors and officers, sailed from England, around the world. Coasts were charted, animals sketched and new plant spe__ __ __ __ were collected.

Condit__ __ __s in the "mess" rooms for the crew were atro__ __ __ __ __. The mess sect__ __ __ was dark, smelly and overcrowded. Hammocks were hung from hooks in the beams and the tables were slung by ropes. There was no spec__ __ __ place to wash and no toilet so the crew used buckets. Vic__ __ __ __ fights often broke out between the sailors in the cramped condi__ __ __ __s.

Endeavour Facts

Length:	35 m
Width:	10 m
Depth:	4 m
Weight:	386 ton
Masts:	Three Foremast
	Main Mast
	Mizzen Mast
Height of main mast:	30 m
Complete crew:	94 men

Pace out 35 m by 10 m. (large step = 1 m) and see the size of space ninety-four people lived in for three years.

✪ What is a sea map called? _____

✪ What animals do you think they would have sketched from America? _____

✪ They collected plants from a bay called "Botany Bay." What does botany mean? _____

_____

✪ Why do you think fights broke out among the crew?

_____

e A replica of the Endeavour was built in Western Australia in the 1990s. After a world voyage in 1997, visiting many ports in England, she returned to Sydney, Australia, where people were able to board her and get the feel of how sailors and officers lived.

Would you have liked to voyage on the Endeavour? _____ Why? _____

_____

Title: _____

Admiral Nelson's "great" cabin

gun ports on HMS Victory

success

successful

ory

Vict__ __ __

hist__ __ __

mem__ __ __

territ__ __ __

ary

ordin__ __ __

milit__ __ __

station__ __ __

necess__ __ __

ery

discov__ __ __

batt__ __ __

Admiral Nelson joined the British Navy at the age of twelve in 1770. Nelson was a brave man. He lost an eye, then one of his arms in various battles. In 1805, at the suc__ __ __ __ful battle of Trafalgar, he was killed in action.

His flagship Vic__ __ __ __ carried 102 stat__ __ __ __ __ __ guns bolted to the decks. Some guns shot ordin__ __ __ cannon b__ __ __s, but some shot sharp splinters of metal to rip sails. Others had chain shot to damage masts and rigging. Grape shot was necess__ __ __ for a wide spread.

grape shot in canvas bag

The Vict__ __ __'s batt__ __y of guns had a range of up to 3 km.

chain shot

cannon ball

You're an author. Write a primary title and two subtitles for chapters of your book.

_____

_____

_____

_____

_____

_____

⭐ What was Nelson's flag ship called? _____

_____

⭐ In what year was Nelson born? _____

⭐ Why was it necessary to fire off grape shots? _____

_____

⭐ What do you think a "battery of guns" means? _____

_____

e Admiral Lord Horatio Nelson has a place in history. This is one of his famous quotes: "England expects every man to do his duty."
Nelson covered much territory in fighting ships from Canada to Italy in the Mediterranean Sea.
His "Victory" is now open for visitors in Portsmouth, England.
Try writing a description of a sea battle.

Title: _____

pesticides

fungi__ __ __ __

increases

increasing

decreases

decr__ __ __ __ __ __

tion

pollu__ __ __ __

na__ __ __ __al

popula__ __ __ __s

industrializa__ __ __ __

habita__ __ __ __

any more?

_____

_____

_____

Our vast oceans are becoming more and more polluted.

As world popula__ __ __ __s grow, we are dumping huge

quantities of sewage into the oceans. Farmers and gardeners

overuse fertilizers and pesti__ __ __ __ __, which make their

way via rivers to the sea.

Ships dump garbage over the side and factories spew out all sorts of chemicals as

industrial__ __ __ __ __ __ __   incre__ __ __s.

Animals are becoming entangled in old f__ __ __ing nets. Birds are being born with

deformities. Schools of fish are decrea__ __ __ __ in numbers. Seaweeds are dying.

What are the solu__ __ __ __s? How can we save this place of

habita__ __ __ __ for millions of sea creatures and pl__ __ __s?

✪ Name some different types of pollution which

affect our oceans. _____

_____

_____

✪ Think of solutions to save our seas. _____

_____

_____

_____

Design a poster about this page. Give it a title.

_____

_____

_____

_____

e Radioactivity is another pollutant. Some isolated Pacific Islands have been used to test nuclear bombs. For thousands of years they will remain so radioactive that they will be unsafe for human habitation.

Do you think this is right? _____ Why? _____

_____

Title: _____

When oil spills on water, it spreads out and covers the surface. Put a drop of cooking oil on a bowl of water.

ALASKA

Anchorage

oil slick

zeros	
5 hundred	500
5 thousand	5,000
5 million	5,000,000
or	

w__ __ld

w__ __st

w__ __ry

w__ __king

w__ __th

w__ __ds

One of the w__ __ld's wo__st oil spills happened in March 1989. The super tanker "Exxon Valdez," carrying mill__ __ __s of liters of oil ran aground off the South coast of Alaska. Over forty million (40, _____ , _____) liters of crude oil wor__ __ mil__ __ __ __s of dollars spilled into the sea.

As the oil slick spread, animals, birds and fish died in thous__ __ __s. Fish suffocated as gills were blocked by __ __ __. Birds covered by oil could no longer fl__ __t or fly. Sea otters with oil-clogged fur could not keep warm and died from the cold. Many marine creatures died of poisoning as they licked or pecked at the o__ __.

oil-soaked feathers

oil-clogged fur on sea otters

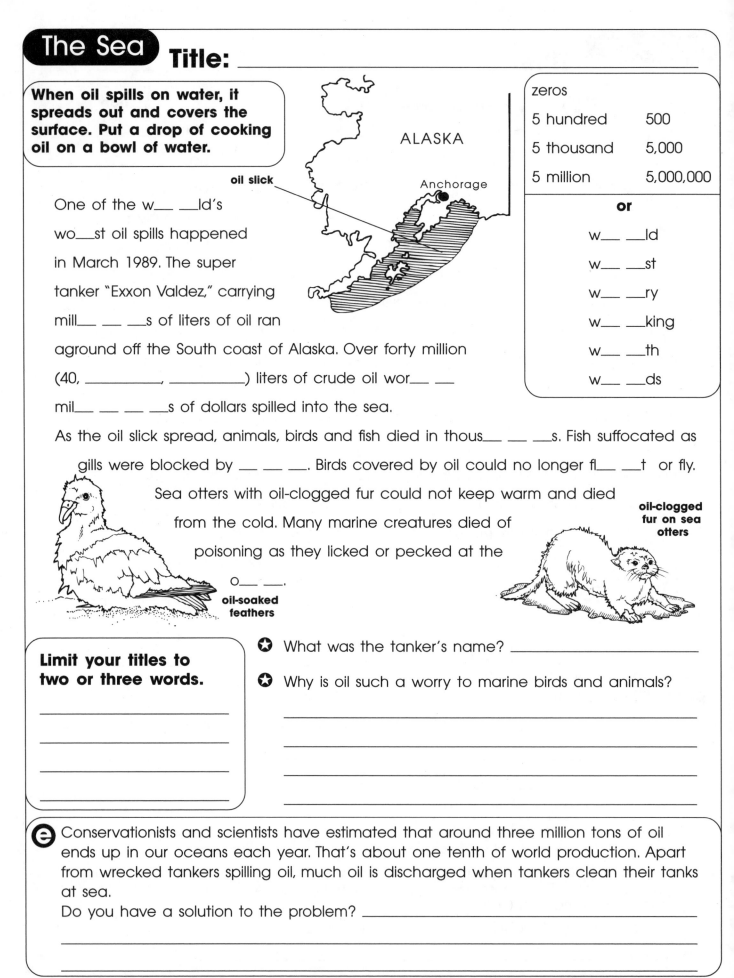

Limit your titles to two or three words.

_____
_____
_____
_____

⭐ What was the tanker's name? _____

⭐ Why is oil such a worry to marine birds and animals?

_____
_____
_____
_____

e Conservationists and scientists have estimated that around three million tons of oil ends up in our oceans each year. That's about one tenth of world production. Apart from wrecked tankers spilling oil, much oil is discharged when tankers clean their tanks at sea.

Do you have a solution to the problem? _____
_____

The Sea

Title: _____

layers of bodies of marine creatures and plants

rock layers

designed

chemicals

decay

__ __ __ __ __ing

cover

__ __ __ __ __ed

lubricate

__ __ __ __ __ __ __ __ __ḙing

trap

__ __ __ __ped

Oil is often found in the rocky floor of our oceans.
When tiny marine creatures die, they drift to the oc__ __ __ floor. Over millions of years,
the layers of dec__ __ __ng plant and animal matter are cov__ __ __ __ by sand and
mud, which form into r__ __k layers. The trap__ __ __ bodies form a dark, sticky
substance between r__ __ __ lay__ __ __. This is oil.

Oil is important to people. It keeps our cars running.
It keeps our planes in the a__ __. It is used for
lub__ __ __ __ __ing working parts of engines.
Some heaters are des__ __ __ed to use oil and oil helps us make
electric power. O__ __ is also mixed with chem__ __ __ __ __ to
make plastics.

oil layer   rock layer

rock layer

⭐ Where is the sticky oil found? _____

_____

Design a poster about oil. Give it a title.

_____

_____

_____

_____

⭐ Where does the oil come from originally? (What is
it made from?) _____

_____

⭐ Write some uses for oil. _____

_____

_____

e Oil is also found in the hot desert areas of the Middle East. This area was originally
beneath the waves when the oil was formed. The ocean floor has been pushed up to
form land and so now you can see oil rigs drilling through sand down to the bedrock
and pools of oil.
Look in your atlas for Iraq, Iran and other countries in the Middle East.

Title: _____

built

b__ __ __ding

supply

supplies

machinery
engines
winches

derrick mast

floating oil rig

helipad

crane

sleeping/eating

sea level

ballast feet

shallow
water rig

mass

m__ __ __ive

reserve

re__ __ __ __ǿoirs

individual

__ __ __ __vidually

stable

s__ __ __ility

Most oil is found deep in the ocean bedrock. Mass__ __ __ oil rigs are b__ __lt to drill through the rock to the oil res__ __ __ __ __rs.
In shallow water, the steel legs of the rig are jacked down notch by n__ __ __ __ indiv__ __ __ __ __ __ __ until the rig is standing in a level position.

In deep water, the o__ __ r__ __ floats and is wei__ __ed down by huge feet filled with sea water as ballast to provide stab__ __ __ __ __. Both these types of rig have plat__ __ __ __s above the waves on which people work and live. They also have heli__ __ __s so that crew and sup__ __ __ __s can be flown to and f__ __ __ shore.

✪ What is an oil rig mainly used for? _____

_____

✪ Why do they jack the legs down individually? _____

_____

_____

Supply a couple of titles.

_____

_____

_____

_____

✪ What supplies do you think would be needed? _____

_____

_____

e Drill bits are the cutting teeth at the end of the drill shaft. These are rotated to drill through hard rock. Steel bits are studded with industrial diamonds so they stay

sharp. Try to find out why diamonds are used. _____

_____

_____

Comprehension Lifters – Book 4   World Teachers Press®

Title: _____

The most feared creature in the oce__ __ is the shark. There are several different spe__ __es of shark and one of the most effi__ __ __ __t hunters is the great white,

which grows to about 6 meters. (How tall are you? _____ cm.) The heaviest great white ever caught weighed over 1,500 kg. (How heavy are you? _____ kg.)

Sharks have several rows of sharp t__ __th, which keep grow__ __ __ all their lives. They eat almost anything from fish to marine mammals such as dolph__ __ __. People swimming offer an easy meal to a hu__ __ __y shark as they have no spe__ __al defense such as speed, stingers, long teeth, or sh__ __p claws.

ci like sh

spe__ __al

vi__ __ous

deli__ __ous

effi__ __ent

spe__ __es

ce like sh

o__ __an

Write a frightening title.

_____

_____

Write a non-frightening one.

_____

_____

• Choose one to write at the top of the page.

✪ What was the mass of the heaviest great white shark ever caught? _____

✪ What is special about shark teeth? _____

_____

✪ An average great white grows to 6 meters. How many times longer is it than you? _____

✪ Does it matter if a shark damages or loses some teeth? _____ Does it matter if you lose a tooth? _____ Why? _____

🅮 The film "Jaws" and its sequels show the fear of sharks and how we think of them as vicious killers.

However, shark attacks are actually few and far between with more sharks being killed by human beings.

Do you think the shark's reputation is correct? _____ Why? _____

_____

_____

Title: _____

ue

bl__ __

contin__ __

cl__ __

purs__ __

resc__ __

val__ __

arg__ __

tiss__ __

scientist

muscle

a cruising shark

amazing

astounding

surp__ __ __ing

extraordinary

aston__ __ __ing

_____

_____

Most fish swim day and night without stopping.

Amaz __ __ __ly, they conti__ __ __ swimming their

whole lives. It is surp__ __ __ __ __ __ that they can

keep this up without becoming tired.

To find cl__ __s about this aston__ __ __ __ __ __ feature of fish, sci__ __ __ __sts

have examined the muscle tiss__ __ and have found two types of mus__ __ __.

The "red" mus__ __ __s are crisscrossed with hundreds of blood

vessels to supply continuous energy and oxygen.

So, the fish is able to keep on swimming.

red muscle

The "white" m__ __ __ __ __ tissue does not have

many bl__ __d vess__ __s and is used for

short bursts of speed to purs__ __

dinner, or avoid being dinner for

another hungry mouth.

★ What does "fish swim day and night" mean?

_____

_____

★ Why do you think some muscles are called

"red" muscles? _____

_____

Keep your two titles to five words or less.

_____

_____

_____

_____

★ "To avoid being dinner." What does this mean?

_____

_____

e The reason that most fish must keep swimming is twofold. First, the gills must have water, with oxygen, flowing through them so that the fish can "breathe." Second, so the fish does not sink or float to the top of the water but maintains its comfortable level.

Why is "breathe" in quotes? _____

_____

Comprehension Lifters – Book 4

Title: _____

dorsal fins

tuna

sea horse

dorsal fin

pectoral fin

wr
— —ap
— —ist
— —iggle
— —ithing
— —ecks
— —ong

Sea creatures move in many different ways. The eel __ __iggles its way

through the water with a writh__ __ __ movement like a snake. The

sea horse ripples its dor__ __ __ fin to thrust it forward. The octopus can __ __ap its

tentacles around seaweeds or bits of shipwr__ __ __ __ to pull it along or it can simply

grip with its sucker pads.

manta ray

It might be wro__ __ to say that the huge manta ray swims, as it

seems to "fly" through the water flapping its enlarged

pect__ __ __ __ fins like wings.

A swordfish can swim at speeds of 85 kilometers

per hour. Sometimes they collide with small boats

and their "sword" can pierce wooden planking.

writhing eel

✪ Which creature wriggles and writhes? _____

_____

Write two titles describing the main idea of the page.

_____

_____

_____

_____

✪ Why might it be wrong to say a manta ray

swims? _____

_____

✪ Where is the dorsal fin? _____

✪ Where is the pectoral fin? _____

e Tails and bodies wave and provide a fish with forward thrust. Pectoral fins paddle and provide lift so the fish does not sink. Some fish, like the pike, have a gas bladder they can inflate or deflate. Some flat fish gulp water and eject it through their gills, like being jet-propelled.

Why does a pike inflate its gas bladder? _____

_____

Title: _____

tasty morsels

species
incubate
hatchling
venture
scurry
reptiles
marine
aquatic
morsels

Turtles are rept_ _ _ _ that live most of their lives in the sea. They are called marine reptiles. The female turtles vent_ _ _ onto land to lay e_ _ _ in sandy mounds. The turtle then leaves the eggs to inc_ _ _ _ _ and hatch on their own.

To birds, hat_ _ _ _ _g turtles are tender, tasty mors_ _ _, so they scu_ _ _ over the sand and down to the water before hungry birds can snap them up.

Once in the water, their troubles are not over as larger fish enjoy a meal of baby turtle also. Turtles eat fish, worms, prawns and some plants and insects. Baby turtles eat the same, but tiny species.

Choose the best title.

☐ Marine Reptiles

☐ Turtles

☐ Tasty Morsels

☐ Baby Turtles

☐ What Turtles Eat

• Write it at the top of the page.

✪ Turtles are called marine reptiles.

| True | False | Doesn't say |

✪ There are two main dangers for baby turtles. What are they?_____

_____

✪ What do baby turtles eat? _____

_____

ⓔ Terrapin is the usual name given to the aquatic freshwater turtle. Tortoise is the usual name for the terrestrial (land-based) species. The shell has two sections. The hard upper shell is called the carapace and the softer undershell is called the plastron. The two

shells are joined at the sides. Why? _____

_____

Title: _____

tele = far off, at a distance

telegraph

__ __ __ __phone

__ __ __ __vision

__ __ __ __scope

North Star

horizon

latitude scale on central rod

cross-staff in use

tion

naviga__ __ __ __

destina__ __ __ __

calcula__ __ __ __

posi__ __ __ __s

inven__ __ __ __

na__ __ __ __al

direc__ __ __ __

compass

Early sailors had no radio-t__ __ __phones or satellites to help navig__ __ __ __ __. Charts were inexact or non-existent. But captains still had to know their posi__ __ __ __ __ at sea to reach their destin__ __ __ __ __s.

By the 12th century, many ships carried a compass with a magnetized needle that always pointed North. In the 16th cent__ __ __, navigators had the benefit of a cross-staff which was pointed at the North Star and the horizon. This gave "latitude."

lines of latitude

equator   **0°**

By the 17th c__ __ __ __ __ __, most ships had a t__ __ __scope which helped identify headlands or islands.

In the 18th century, the inven__ __ __ __ of "chronometers" (early clocks) helped in their calcul__ __ __ __n of longitude.

lines of longitude

Choose the best title which tells the main idea.

☐ 16th and 17th Centuries

☐ Telescopes

☐ Early Navigation Instruments

☐ Sailors of Long Ago

✪ What helped navigators find the right direction in the 12th century? _____

_____

✪ How did a telescope help? _____

_____

✪ Why do you think maps were inexact in the old days?

_____

_____

ℯ The invention of the sextant in the mid-18th century made navigation much easier and more accurate. The sextant consisted of a series of mirrors which the navigator lined up with the sun and the horizon. The latitude could then be read off the scale. What do you think would be a disadvantage about the use of the sextant?

_____

_____

Title: _____

magnet
magnetized

two
whole
write

tape

slice of cork

You'll need:

- a needle
- a magnet
- a cork
- tape
- round plastic ice-cream container

magnet N

needle

You can make your own instruments for navig_ _ _ _ _. A working comp_ _ _ is easy to make. First, stroke a ne_ _le with a magnet. (Always go the same way, not backwards and for_ _ _ _ _.) Now your needle is magn_ _ _ _ed. Tape it to a cork slice. (A sl_ _ _ floats flatter than a whole cork.)

compass

Print compass points on to the sides of your plastic cont_ _ _er. (If you're using a good bowl, you can print comp_ _ _ poi_ _s on a ring of cardboard.)

Now, float your new com_ _ _s on the water in your bowl or contai_ _ _. When it comes to rest, gently move the bowl around until the n_ _ _ _ _ points to N_ _ _ _.

⭐ After collecting all the things you need, what would you do first? _____

_____

_____

⭐ What is the next step? _____

_____

_____

⭐ Then what? _____

_____

_____

Write two titles.

_____

_____

_____

_____

shortest shadow
at noon

e You can also find out when local noon occurs. Stick a post in the ground and mark the end of the shadow. After a while mark the end again. The shadow will shorten until noon and then lengthen again. (Note that local noon where you are now may not be the same as 12 o'clock on your watch.)

Title: _____

sword

cutlass

flint lock

ea

h__ __d

d__ __dly

w__ __pons

__ __rlier

inst__ __d

h__ __vy

l__ __d

__ __rnings

Around 200 years ago, the "Men of War" fighting ships had many

h__ __vy cannons to sink and destroy enemy vessels. But when

pirates boarded their ships, sailors needed other w__ __pons, such as

pistols and cutlasses.

A cut__ __ __ __ was a curved s__ __rd with razor-sharp edg__ __.

It was d__ __dly and could slice off an arm or even a h__ __d.

Around the 1680s (about _____ years ago)

the flint lock pistol was inven__ __ __. It had

a safety lock which was a great advance on

__ __rlier pistols. People made their own bullets

(round shot) by heating l__ __d until it melted

and pouring it into a hollow mold.

hollow mold for
making round shot

Choose the best headline.

☐ Razor Sharp

☐ Men of War

☐ New Weapon at Sea

☐ Hollow Molds

⭐ What were the hand weapons sailors used?

_____

⭐ Why was the flint lock pistol better than earlier

pistols? _____

_____

⭐ How did people make bullets? _____

_____

e It took time to load a flint lock pistol.

1. Set the safety lock to "half cock."
2. Pour gunpowder down the barrel.
3. Ram a musket ball down the barrel with a "ramrod."
4. Pour a small amount of gun powder into the "priming pan" and close cover.
5. Set the safety lock to "full cock" – then fire.

What does it mean when we say, "Don't go off half-cocked"? _____

_____

Title: _____

variety
answered
discipline

dis or ful

__ __ __honest

color__ __ __

__ __ __obedient

pain__ __ __

usual

un__ __ __ __ __

On crowded sailing ships, there were discip__ __ __ __ problems. Some sailors fought with each other. Some were __ __ __hon__ __ __ and stole things and some were __ __ __obed__ __ __ __ and ans__ __ __ed back.

A var__ __ __ __ of punishments was ordered by the captain or officers. The most usu__ __ pun__ __ __ __ __ __t was the "checked shirt." An offender would be tied to the mast or rigging and lashed. The lashes tore the skin, showing lines of blood in a crisscross pattern like a col__ __ful shirt.

leg irons punishment

The lashes were so pain__ __ __ that sailors often fainted. For a small offense, sailors could be put in leg irons and left in the blazing sun or lashing rain.

✪ What were some of the discipline problems? _____

_____

Write two titles.

_____

_____

_____

_____

✪ What was a "checked shirt"? _____

_____

_____

✪ How do you think "leg irons" worked? _____

_____

e Keelhauling was very cruel. A sailor would be hauled underneath the ship and up the other side. Barnacles (sharp shells on the hull) tore at their skin and often men drowned.

Keelhauling was outlawed on all naval vessels. Why? _____

_____

The Sea

Title: _____

Marie Celeste under full sail

son

daughter

Word bank
mystery
mysteries
abandoned
deserted
solved
solution
craft
vessel
struggle
violence

Here is one of the great sea myst__ __ __ __ __ which has never been sol__ __ __. What happened to the captain and crew of the Marie Celeste?

The M__ __ __ __ C__ __ __ __ __ __ __ was a two-masted American cargo ves__ __ __ with square sails. She set sail on Nov__ __ __ __ __ __ 7, 1872, from New York bound for Genoa, Italy with a full cargo. She also carried a crew of seven, plus the captain, his wife and baby dau__ __ __ __ __.

A month later she was found ab__ __ __oned off the coast of Portugal. The cra__ __ was des__ __ __ed. There was no sign of a strug__ __ __ or viol__ __ __ __. The cargo was intact and there was money still on board.

Write three mysterious titles.

_____

_____

_____

_____

_____

_____

- Write the best one at the top of the page.

✪ When did the vessel leave New York?_____

✪ What do you think "two-masted" means?_____
_____

✪ What does "square rigged" mean?
_____
_____

✪ Did the crew leave because of a fight? _____
What was your clue/s? _____
_____
_____

e The final entry in the captain's log was just routine at 8 a.m. November 25. The ship was seaworthy and there was a half-written letter left by one of the crew. Perhaps you have a theory of what might have happened.

_____

_____

_____

Title: _____

known
dishonest

pirate ships were small and fast

large merchant ship

| costly |
| precious |
| valuable |
| prized |
| treasure |
| dear |

| **cious** |
| suspi__ __ __ __ __ |
| pre__ __ __ __ __ |
| atro__ __ __ __ __ |

Preci__ __ __ cargo was often carried from one country to another by sea. There were valuab__ __ gold coins, silver plate and diamonds.

Disho__ __ __ __ sailors thought that all this trea__ __ __ __ could be theirs for the taking. They would attack and board ships known to be carrying cos__ __ __ cargo, fighting the crew until the ship was theirs.

walking the plank

These were the pirates of the high seas.

Pi__ __ __ __ __ used the ships they captured to chase after other treas__ __ __ ships. By flying the normal flag they could sail quite close before the merchant ship became

susp__ __ __ __us. Then up went every piece of canvas and the race was on to capture the pri__ __ __ cargo.

✪ Who were the dishonest raiders at sea?_____

_____

"Pirates" would be a good title – but dull. Think of some interesting titles.

_____

_____

_____

_____

✪ What do you think these mean?

"theirs for the taking"_____

_____

"every piece of canvas" _____

_____

e The skull and crossbones became the most feared flag on the high seas. Pirate raids were often carried out with atrocious cruelty. Sailors faced sharp cutlasses or they were made to "walk the plank" with hands bound so they would drown. Sailing ships carried more and more sails so they could escape the raiders, but pirate ships were small and fast.

Title: _____

Draw the treasure map here.

ough

r__ __ __ __ly

t__ __ __ __

en__ __ __ __

f__ __ __ __t

ight

e__ __ __ __y

l__ __ __ __ly

we__ __ __ __y

f__ __ __ __ing

One day Pirate Pete was captured. He quickly ate his map of where he had hidden ei__ __ __y pieces of gold. Later, he escaped. Help him redraw his map.

anchor

treasure chest

He remem__ __ __ __ __ that the map of the island was rou__ __ly a 14 cm by 6 cm rectangle with each centimeter equal to one kilometer. He recal__ __ __ that the island was widest from east to w__ __ __. He could see in his mind's eye the sandy bay to the north where he had an__ __ __ __ed his ship, and the hi__ __ hill to the south-west.

re mem ber ed
remembered
re call ed
recalled

He rem__ __ __ __ __ed the tou__ __ time he had dragging the wei__ __ty chest of gold 4 km to the cave on the east side of the hill where he piled enou__ __ rocks on the chest to cover it.

This page ought to have a title. Think of three.

_____

_____

_____

_____

_____

✪ What was in Pirate Pete's treasure chest? _____

_____

✪ What do you think "he could see it in his mind's eye" means?_____

_____

✪ Do you think he ever got his eighty pieces of gold back? _____ Write a short story about it.

The Sea   Title: _____

Arctic tern with a large wing span for long journeys

North
_ _ _ _ern
South
_ _ _ _ _ _ _

Arctic
Ant arc tic
Ant_ _ _ _ _ _ _a

migra
_ _ _ _ _nt
_ _ _ _ _te
_ _ _ _ _ting
_ _ _ _ _tion

maybe
perhaps
possibly
possibility

One of the wonders of the bird world is the mig_ _ _ion of the Arctic tern. It is a small bird and breeds in the Ar_ _ _ _ during the short no_ _ _ern summer. Once the days grow shorter and colder the t_ _ _s start their long mi_ _ _ _ _ _n. They fly over land and over the oceans until they reach South Africa, S_ _ _ _ America or Antar_ _ _ _a for the brief s_ _ _ _ern summer. The round trip for the tern mig_ _ _ _ _ _ is 35,000 kilometers.

Swans in V formation

No one really knows how birds find their way. Poss_ _ _y they learn from older birds. Ma_ _ _ they know the way by instinct. Per_ _ _ _ they can navigate by the sun or the stars. It's a pos_ _ _ _ _ _ty they use all of these methods.

★ How far does the Arctic tern fly in a year? _____

_____

★ Where does this tern lay its eggs and raise its chicks?

_____

★ Which method do you think birds use to find their way?

_____

Why do you think that? _____

_____

Write two possible titles. Choose your best for the top of the page.

_____
_____
_____
_____

ⓔ Heavy bird migrants such as geese and swans fly in "V" formations. Each bird receives help from the wing-flap of the bird ahead. Wing-flaps move the air and reduce "drag" for the bird behind. The lead bird has no help so tires quickly. This is why the lead changes every few kilometers.